GIFTS

OF

HEALING

God's healing Power to destroy sicknesses and diseases

SAMUEL O. OREFUWA

All scripture quotations are from King James Version of the bible except stated

Direct quotations from the bible are in italics.

All rights reserved

Gifts of Healing

ISBN 978-0-6399827-2-4

Copyright 2018

Samuel O. Orefuwa

All rights reserved. No potion of this book maybe reproduced without written permission from the publisher.

For further information & permission write to
Word of Faith Media & Publications
311 Arcadia Centre
179 Steve Biko rd
Arcadia
Pretoria
0083
Republic of South Africa

info@wof-ministries.com
www.wof-ministries.com

Contents

Chapter 1:   Do not be ignorant

Chapter 2:   Outpouring of the Anointing

Chapter 3:   Healing Anointing

Chapter 4:   Present your body

Chapter 5:   Behave your faith

Chapter 6:   Believe you were healed

Chapter 7:   Manifestations of Healing Gifts

Chapter 8:   Christ the Healer

Chapter 9:   Seek God & worship Him

Chapter 10: Love walk

Samuel O. Orefuwa

Chapter 1
Do not be Ignorant

Ignorance can cost you your life or make your life miserable.

"My people are destroyed for lack of knowledge: because thou hast rejected knowledge." Hosea 4:6

"They know not, neither will they understand; they walk on in darkness: all the foundations of the earth are out of course." Psalm 82:5

If you are ignorant of God's healing power, it can cost you your life or that of your loved ones. I have seen many who were ignorant of God's healing power die of diseases especially those who belong to Jesus, for whom He paid the price for His power to be their inheritance

Gifts of Healing

and to use that same power to destroy sicknesses and diseases that attacks their bodies and their loved ones.

Satan is mean and wicked, he steals, kills and destroys using diseases as his weapon if you allow him, but when you come against him with God's healing power, he runs away and leaves you alone. You cannot afford to be ignorant of God's healing power that is available for the church. You need to study the bible and see it operate in Jesus' ministry and desire to see the same work in your body. The Jesus in the Bible is still alive! He lives in you since you have received Him as Lord and Saviour. He is in you with all of the power of God that you will need in life.

"Now concerning spiritual gifts, brethren, I would not have you ignorant." (1 Corinthians 12:1)

Verse 7, "But the manifestation of the Spirit is given to every man to profit withal."

Verse 9, "To another faith by the same Spirit; to another the gifts of healing by the same Spirit."

God wants you to know of His provisions for you; He doesn't want you to be ignorant of His divine healing power to demolish sicknesses and diseases. He says in 1 Corinthians 12:1, "Now concerning spiritual gifts, brethren, I would not have you ignorant." I would not have you ignorant because it could cost you a lot. He has made His spiritual gifts available for the church and His spiritual gifts are given to meet all the various needs of the church. No matter your need, one of the gifts will meet that need, they are the blessings of Christ for the church. If you study them, teach them, pray about them and desire their manifestations as a church, they will manifest. There is so much power deposited in the spiritual realm for people to draw from. God has different kinds of power to meet different human needs.

"And God hath set some in the church, first apostles, secondarily prophets, thirdly teachers, after that miracles, then gifts of healings, helps, governments, diversities of tongues."(1 Corinthians 12:28)

The almighty God has set in His church some people through whom His healing power flows. This flow He called "Gifts of healings". Gifts of healings are gifts of Christ to His body. Healing power is a gift to the church and with this gift you are able to destroy the enemy of sickness and diseases. It is God's provision to make your body healthy and strong, free of sicknesses and diseases that weaken the human body. When He said He has set some in His church, it means there are those whom He has set in His church with mighty healing power to heal the sick both in the church and outside the church. This is an act of His love for His people. Praise God!

Seek for more knowledge of how the gifts of healing work, take advantage of them for yourself and for your loved ones. This gift operates in my life and has helped me for my health, my wife and children including my parents. It is a blessed gift

Gifts of Healing

of heaven to the church. When in operation it brings relief to the sick. What a loving God we serve.

Chapter 2
The Outpouring of the Anointing

"While Peter yet spake these words, the Holy Ghost fell on all them which heard the word." (Acts 10: 44)

The Lord God Almighty is pouring out His Spirit on all people, both the Jews and Gentiles. Here, in the above scriptures, He has poured out His Spirit on the Gentiles after the visitation of Cornelius in which he was directed to seek for Peter for what he was hungry for. He was a Gentile who fasted a lot and was generous and when God was satisfied with his hunger, He sent an angel to him to direct him to Peter who will lead him to Christ, the Saviour. It was while Peter was speaking to Cornelius and his family that the Holy Ghost was poured out on him, his family and friends. God's presence fell on them and they began to speak in tongues.

God is still pouring out His Holy Spirit on hungry people. If you hunger and thirst for His presence and power, He will open the spirit realm over you and pour out His power on you. A decade ago, I was talking and praying on the offering in our church, while praying I just felt the heavens open over me and the presence and power of God fell on me and the church. There was great manifestations of power on the church that day! I know heavens do open and the Holy Ghost can be poured out on people, I have experienced that many times. All you need to do is to just show Him how hungry you are for His presence and power like Cornelius. Cornelius was a religious man given to fasting and why was he fasting? He was hungry for God. God saw that and led him to a spiritual guide who would open him up to His plan of salvation in Christ.

"And when the day of Pentecost was fully come, they were all with one accord in one place." Acts 2:1

Christ had told the disciples to stay in Jerusalem, Acts 1:4, and wait for the outpouring of the Holy Spirit. They obeyed and were in one place praying, Acts 1:14, then in Acts 2:2 the heavens over them opened and the Holy Ghost and power was poured on them. Apostle Peter, in Acts 2:16, explained what happened to them. Peter unfolded God's plan for the last days and one of the signs of the end times is an outpouring of the Holy Ghost. God's Spirit is being poured out on all human beings that are hungry and thirsty for Him.

We are in the last days of God's glory and power flowing out of heaven onto human beings whose hearts are open to be filled. The Holy Spirit is here on the earth, He was promised by the Father, Jesus paid the ultimate price and the Holy

Spirit is here raining on the earth on all flesh. This outpouring is the anointing of God being poured out on the earth to empower God's people, to free them from various bondages and destroy the work of the enemy on the earth. Among this outpouring is God's healing anointing being poured out from the realm of the spirit to destroy the yoke of sickness and disease. Prophet Isaiah spoke of this anointing:

"And it shall come to pass in that day, that his burden shall be taken away from off thy shoulder, and his yoke from off thy neck, and the yoke shall be destroyed because of the anointing." (Isaiah 10:27)

Sicknesses and diseases are yokes of the enemy and God is pouring out His healing anointing to destroy these yokes on people. He loves His people, He does not want them sick or diseased hence, the outpouring of His anointing to destroy sicknesses.

"The Spirit of the Lord is upon me, because he hath anointed me to preach the gospel to the poor; He hath sent me to heal the broken hearted, to preach deliverance to the captives, and recovering of sight to the blind, to set at liberty them that are bruised." (Luke 4:18)

The purpose of the Spirit upon Jesus Christ was to heal, deliver and recover God's people who were under the attack of the enemy. The healing anointing was on Christ and He went about to heal, deliver and recover people from the oppression of the devil.

"How God anointed Jesus of Nazareth with the Holy Ghost and with power: who went about doing good, and healing all that were oppressed of the devil; for God was with him." (Acts 10:38)

From the above scripture we see how Jesus Christ was anointed with the Spirit and power to minister healing to those OPPRESSED of the devil. This is the summary of Christ's ministry while He was on the earth. Jesus had the healing anointing on Him without measure therefore there was no sickness and diseases He could not heal. "For God giveth not the spirit by measure unto him." (John 3:34)

Christ had the anointing on Him including the healing anointing without measure. The words 'Spirit anointing' and 'Holy Ghost power' are synonymous terms so when the bible says He gives the Spirit, it also means the anointing was given to Christ without measure. However, those of us with the ministry gifts of Christ, sent to do specific work in the body, have limited measures of the Spirit or anointing to heal. Some, called into the healing ministry, manifest the anointing for certain diseases consistently while they hardly see some other diseases healed in their ministry. It is Christ that is anointing men as He wills but, in limited measures. It is raining time, both the latter and former rain are falling; seek Christ for a fresh outpouring on your life. You need fresh oil and it's available; His spirit is raining on all flesh in these last days.

Chapter 3
The Healing Anointing

Let's study the healing anointing in the ministry of Jesus.

"And the whole multitude sought to touch him: for there went virtue out of him, and healed them all." (Luke 6:19)

Multitudes came to Christ to hear and be healed of their diseases as they sought to touch Him. Why did they seek to touch Him? It's because they knew healing power was flowing out of Him. How did they know? They must have heard and seen the healing power of God at work and people getting healed. They were driven by what they heard and sought to touch Him, knowing that whatever was healing the sick was flowing from Him strongly and that by just touching Christ they will be healed without Him praying for them. The scripture says virtue went out of Him. That virtue is the healing power of God healing them who came to Jesus in response to their faith.

"And a certain woman, which had an issue of blood twelve

years, And had suffered many things of many physicians, and had spent all that she had, and was nothing bettered, but rather grew worse, When she had heard of Jesus, came in the press behind, and touched his garment. For she said, If I may touch but his clothes, I shall be whole. And straightway the fountain of her blood was dried up; and she felt in her body that she was healed of that plague. And Jesus, immediately knowing in himself that virtue had gone out of him, turned him about in the press, and said, who touched my clothes?" (Mark 5:25-30)

The woman in the above scripture was healed because she heard of Jesus (v. 27) and acted on what she heard. What did she hear? Definitely she must have heard that Jesus was anointed with healing power and that many were getting healed in His ministry. She did not come to Jesus to seek an audience with Him or to have Him pray for her, but rather she acted on what she heard. She said to herself: "If I may but touch His clothes I shall be healed." (v28) The question is why she didn't say: "If Jesus can just pray for me I shall be made whole" but instead she said "If I may touch but His clothes". She must have known or heard that something was on Him that was healing the sick and whatever that was on Him healing the sick must also be on His clothes hence she went after His clothes.

In verse 29, "straightway the fountain of her blood was dried up; and she felt in her body that she was healed of that plague." What did she feel? She felt relieved of the symptoms of her disease. The healing power of God brought that relief. In verse 30, Jesus, immediately knowing in Himself that virtue had gone out of Him, turned Him about in the press, and said, who touched my clothes?" Jesus also felt something, He felt virtue go out from Him. The word virtue used in this verse means 'inherent power'. The inherent power in Christ came out of Him and went into the woman. The woman felt the work of this healing power as it brought her relief and Jesus felt it came out of Him. We need to study more on the characteristics of this power that healed this woman as both of them felt the healing power of God.

Characteristics of the Healing Anointing

1. It is transferable or transmittable.

Healing anointing is God's healing power and studying how the woman with the issue of blood was healed shows that the woman took advantage of the character of the anointing of God on Jesus by co-operating with that anointing when she said within herself that if she touches the clothes, she shall be healed. This happened because the healing anointing is transferable. If the anointing was not transferable, an ordinary touch of Jesus' clothes would not have produced any results, but because the anointing can be transferred from certain materials or persons to another, it made that possible. In verse 30 Jesus knew virtue had gone out of Him, that virtue is God's healing anointing on Christ that went out of Him to the woman and she felt the workings of that anointing in her body.

Years ago while I was ministering, someone came out to touch my suit, as soon as they touched my suit, the power of God went through them like electricity. Sometimes I asked my assistants to bring their hands and when I lay my hands on their hands transferring the gifts of healing in my right hand to them to help me pray for the sick, they get healed. I do that a lot especially when my wife is ministering to the sick with me. This is only possible because of the character of the anointing that it is transferable or transmittable. It's because of this character of the healing anointing that makes me pray on handkerchiefs and transfer the healing anointing into it by praying on it until it is soaked with the healing power on me. Whenever the handkerchief is laid on the sick, the sick get healed in Jesus name.

2. It is tangible

Another character of the anointing that we see in Mark 5:25-30 is that the anointing is tangible, meaning it is capable of being touched and felt. The woman touched Jesus' clothes and the healing power of Christ was received by the woman and she felt relieved of the symptoms of her disease. Jesus knew that power had went out of His body, He felt the out flow of power to a recipient because of the tangibility of that power. In Luke 6:9, multitudes sought to touch Him because of the tangibility of the anointing. Why would multitudes want to touch Him if nothing was happening to those who initially touched Him out of curiosity? When healing was coming out of their touch they must have gone to town to tell others saying I touched Him and I was healed by touching Him.

3. It can be stored

As we study certain scriptures, further we see that certain materials conduct and can also absorb the healing anointing which shows another character of the anointing that can be stored, let's look at certain scriptures in the bible that reveal how power was stored.

"And God wrought special miracles by the hands of Paul: So that from his body were brought unto the sick handkerchiefs or aprons, and the diseases departed from them, and the evil spirits went out of them." (Acts 19:11-12)

The anointing on Apostle Paul was transferred to handkerchiefs and those handkerchiefs stored the power of God until they came in contact with sick and diseased people. In Mark 5, the woman with the issues of blood only touched the cloth of Jesus and not His body, meaning Jesus' cloth also stored the anointing that was on Him thus clothes, aprons and handkerchiefs can absorb the healing power of God. We can pray on them and when taken to sick people especially those that are far from us and find it's impossible to travel to where we are, we can send handkerchiefs stored with the healing power of God to them and when it comes in contact with diseased bodies, they get healed.

Chapter 4
Present Your Body

Thank God for Christ's healing gifts to the church. His healing anointing is a gift to the church to destroy the works of the enemy in sick bodies. Is your body under the attack of the enemy? There is a gift for you in the Word of God, it's the healing power of Christ. You have to come to Christ and present your body to Him so He can fill you with His healing power.

"I beseech you therefore, brethren, by the mercies of God, that ye present your bodies a living sacrifice, holy, acceptable unto God, which is your reasonable service." Romans 12:1

God wants you to have a healthy body, full of life and strength, filled with His spirit. He says let your body be a sacrifice, holy and an acceptable body unto God. A sick body is not acceptable to God; it does not glorify Him. But a strong and healthy body is acceptable to God and to have that your body needs to be filled with God's healing power by the Holy Spirit. He has paid the price for you to have a strong and healthy body. He has given you the Holy Spirit to reside in you. He says

"What? Know ye not that your body is the temple of the Holy Ghost which is in you, which ye have of God, and ye are not your own? For ye are bought with a price: therefore, glorify God in your body, and in your spirit, which are God's." (1 Corinthians 6:19)

Your body belongs to God and you have to make your body glorify God. Being filled with sicknesses and diseases does not glorify God. The scripture says your body is the temple of the Holy Spirit and your body has been bought with a price. That price being the stripes of Jesus and the blood of Jesus that redeemed you and the price paid has made available God's Spirit and power to live in your body. Accept this truth, claim the healing power of God to fill your body in Jesus name. Thank the Holy Spirit for renewing the strength of the organs of your body.

Years ago, I started laying hands on my head before I sleep claiming the healing power of God to fill my body with life, strength and energy all night. Saying I believe I will wake up stronger and I got what I asked for, I became stronger! At that time I used to feel weak because I used to spend the day praying for hours and in the evening I would be feeling pain and tiredness but the power of God strengthened me and filled my cells with the life of God when I asked Him to do so. God is faithful to scriptures. Present your body to God, for the life of God to flow into it, for strength and for healing power so that you can glorify God.

"But if the spirit of him that raised up Jesus from the dead dwell in you, he that raised up Christ from the dead shall also quicken your mortal bodies by His spirit that dwelleth in you." (Romans 8:11)

The Holy Ghost comes into you at salvation and you receive His fullness when you are baptized in the Holy Ghost with evidence of speaking in tongues. One of the primary functions of the Holy Ghost in you is to fill your body with life, the life of God called 'Zoë' in Greek. To quicken the body is to fill it with life that life being the strength and power of God. Ask Him today to quicken you, to strengthen you in Jesus name.

Chapter 5
Behave your faith

"And as he entered into a certain village, there met him ten men that were lepers, which stood afar off: And they lifted up their voices, and said, Jesus, Master, have mercy on us. And when He saw them, He said unto them, go shew yourselves unto the priests. And it came to pass, that, as they went, they were cleansed." (Luke 17:12-14)

We are looking at this scripture to see how the lepers were healed by the healing power of God. These lepers saw Jesus and lifted their voices to Jesus to heal them through His mercy. Jesus has a lot of mercy to give out once you can show Him faith. Jesus heard their cries for mercy and responded with an instruction for them "… go show yourselves unto the priests"

The Law concerning lepers

According to the law concerning lepers, in Leviticus 13:2 ,only the priests could confirm them as clean Leviticus 14:2. When the Lord Jesus told them to show themselves to the priest, He was telling them "You are clean" as far as I'm concerned but you have to fulfill the law because when you are clean you have to show yourselves to the priest whose job is to confirm you clean after the necessary sacrifice has been made according to the law concerning lepers in Leviticus 14:5-6, 50-52. These lepers obeyed the instruction of Jesus and headed straight to see the priest whose job is to declare them clean. "...And it came to pass, that, as they went, they were cleansed." They obeyed the instruction of Jesus and while on their way to the priest, they were cleansed. Their leprosy was gone! They had been healed by the healing power of God! Our Lord Jesus, in verse 19, described what happened to one of the lepers who returned to thank Him by saying, "... thy faith hath made thee whole." Jesus put it concisely that the behavior of the lepers was FAITH, that it was their faith that healed them. How do we define this faith that healed these lepers? We can say Faith is behaving the word of God, putting it into action.

The Lepers FAITH

These lepers in their miserable condition covered with sores and scabs with their flesh rotting away as their bodies were desperate for healing. When they heard of Jesus, having heard of him as the Healer and the Messiah who was healing the sick and had healed other lepers, it was in this desperate condition that Jesus told them to go and show themselves to the priest without healing them first. Probably they expected Him to touch them by laying of hands on them or rebuke their condition. He did none of those but just gave them an instruction to behave healed because only cleaned healed lepers must appear before the priest. It's against the law to leave their colony outside the village and to go to the priest in the village claiming that they were cleansed, but rather than question Jesus, they behaved healed and went on to see the priest. As far as Christ was concerned they were cleansed and healed, hence the instruction He gave them to show themselves to the priest. This was a faith test, did they believe what Jesus believed? Yes. They did believe and behaved healed as they went on their way without any hesitation of their miserable condition. It was their behaving healed and cleansed that caused the healing power of God to overwhelm them and clean all of them.

The faith that healed them was their behaving healed because only healed lepers must show up at the priest's house. Their faith pleased God and He poured His healing power on all of them. It is so important that faith must be released if you want anything from God, faith pleases Him and causes Him to manifest His glorious power. Seek God for His Rhema word, His spoken word, whenever you are believing Him for a miracle or healing, get ready to obey His instructions.

At the wedding in Cana of Galilee, Jesus' mother told them to do whatever He would tell them to do. They ran out of wine, at the marriage supper and when Jesus gave them an instruction to fill the water pots with water and serve the guests, they obeyed and as they obeyed Him in serving the guest, wine came out of the water pots instead of water. Jesus' instructions, when obeyed always bring miracles. Seek him for His word, ask Him to show you scriptures, tell Him you will obey Him and His word, if His word says 'you were healed' then behave healed, don't behave sick. He watches over your behavior to see if you believe Him or not.

Proven and Tested Faith

God will prove and test your faith to find out if you really believe. Years ago when my family was believing God for children, I would walk the floor of the house with my bible opened before me and call my wife fruitful. I would say, "'Lord I'm the head of this house and I declare my wife is fruitful, it doesn't matter what the doctor's report says." At the time doctors in London and South Africa said her womb was very sick and can never conceive. I would pray in tongues for hours claiming my children in Jesus name. One day I decided not to go anywhere but to stay indoors seeking God for answer to this problem. I opened all the scriptures on fruitfulness from Genesis and claimed them as talking to me, that according to Mark 11:24, I believe I receive children. After several days of praying in tongues night and day quoting scriptures, suddenly I fell into a trance while praying and an angel stood in front of me and said, "I want to teach you how to pray for your wife". My wife was brought before me and I was shown how to pray for her, the Angel disappeared after showing me what to do. Immediately I called my wife and told her that I had just been visited and was shown how to pray for her.

I did pray for her as I was shown, anointed her womb and called her womb fruitful in Jesus name. Seven days after that visitation my wife called me to tell me she thinks she is pregnant, another journey of faith started because after she conceived, the devil fought the pregnancy. Throughout her conception, she was bleeding, the doctors said she was not pregnant and based on their tests it was just a fibroid, but we both kept declaring she was pregnant. My faith was shaken at one point, I said: "It could be true that you are not pregnant if the doctors and scans can't see the baby after 5months." But my wife's faith was unshaken as she kept declaring she was pregnant and I kept praying in tongues and believing. After nine months of pregnancy the baby was born. Our faith was tested and proven but we prayed in tongues and kept declaring she was pregnant and that the baby is well. God is able to perform the scriptures you believe. You need to show Him the scriptures you are believing and personalize them as yours, calling them done and thanking Him. If you do this and keep at it until He is satisfied with your faith, He will manifest His healing power to you.

Chapter 6
Believe You Were Healed

"Who his own self bare our sins in his own body on the tree, that we, being dead to sins, should live unto righteousness: by whose stripes ye were healed." (1 Peter 2:24)

The truth of God's word concerning diseases was revealed by Apostle Peter when he says "…you were healed". If you were healed then you are healed, its past tense, it has already been done. Jesus has dealt with all sicknesses and diseases and you have to accept the word of God as it is, you have to confront diseases and sicknesses with this truth. The word of God is yours now to act on. Don't vacillate, waiver or wonder on God's truth. He HAS healed you! Prophet Isaiah spoke of your healing in Isaiah 53:5 "…the chastisement of our peace was upon him and with his stripes we are healed."

The prophet saw into the spirit about the sacrifice of Christ and described this vividly in his prophecy what these sufferings would mean to us and proclaimed "…with his stripes we are healed". What the prophet said has been accomplished. You just have to accept it, claim it as yours once you are a believer of Christ. The two scriptures quoted are talking about you, your health and your healing. Don't be in darkness about God's will concerning you. He wants you well, you WERE healed by His pain, wounds and stripes. He took all our sicknesses and diseases on himself that we maybe well.

How To Believe

Your belief system is programmed by what you are hearing and what you have been taught or led to. Apostle Paul wrote in 1 Corinthians 12:2, "Ye know that you were Gentiles, carried away unto these dumb idols, even as ye were led." They believe in idols because they were led into it. Whatever you believe today, you were led to believe one way or the other. It is important that you guard yourself so as not to be misled into believing wrongly. Some are saying there are no more miracles and it's because they were taught to believe so. I was taught to believe in miracles and have seen God do many miracles for me and has used me as a vessel to minister His miracle power to many across the globe. By reading this book, am leading you into believing for your healing or any miracle you desire.

I'm telling you to base your belief on the Word of God, what is written and what has been spoken about your health. When you do that, you are opening yourself for God's mighty healing power to flow through you. God wants His people to believe the Bible. Base your belief on what is written in the

Bible. The Bible has been given to us to know God and His Word and thereby base your belief on His Word. He wants to be believed and when He is pleased with your belief, He will cause you to experience His mighty healing power. When you are sick, you grab hold of your Bible and start searching for scriptures that talk about your healing from Genesis to Revelation and apply them personally. Let the scriptures talk to you personally until they become part of your being. See the Bible as God talking to you. Let Him talk to you as you find scriptures about your healing. Then start thanking Him and accepting whatever He has said as yours, claim the content of the scriptures as yours in Jesus name. Once you have found the scriptures that talk to you start taking your healing, accepting you are healed by His healing power.

Satan the Source of Doubt

Satan will do everything to make you doubt the Bible! Do not allow him to talk to you, reject his suggestions and quote the Bible to him just like Jesus did. He is the source of doubt, the source of attack on your faith and he is also the source of infirmities. The Bible says, in James 4:7 , "Submit yourselves therefore to God, resist the devil, he will flee from you." For sickness to depart, you have to resist Satan's thoughts, suggestions and everything he offers you. Don't take anything from him, he is mean, he wants to steal your life early therefore outsmart him with scriptures. He has stolen many lives and made many to be widows and orphans because he is the source of sorrow. Don't allow Satan into your mind because he is targeting your mind to fill it with doubts and suggestions that you were not healed.

"And, behold, there was a woman which had a spirit of infirmity eighteen years, and was bowed together, and could in no wise lift up herself." (Luke 13:11)

"And ought not this woman, being a daughter of Abraham, whom Satan hath bound, lo, these eighteen years, be loosed from this bond on the Sabbath day?" (Luke 13:16)

For 18 years this woman was bound by the spirit of infirmity, sickness and Jesus said Satan did it. Resist him with scriptures quote them to him, claim the content and benefits of the scriptures you have found as yours and watch how the Holy Spirit inside of you will manifest to perform the scriptures. Remember, to work on yourself to believe the bible first, by searching scriptures that promise you healing and health. In searching for scriptures you may have to engage the Holy Ghost to help you locate relevant scriptures. Years ago I had to pray in tongues for 8 hours asking the Holy Spirit to show me the scripture to use in prayer as we were entering a new year. I did not just want to assume, I asked and He gave me the relevant scripture. He is faithful, search the Bible with Him and He will show you scriptures you have read before but never 'seen'.

Secondly, once you have found the scriptures, claim the content as yours and accept what they are saying. They are the answers to your sickness because the Bible is the book of solutions and answers therefore you must accept the solutions and answers in the scriptures as yours. Thirdly, resist the sickness with the scriptures, and tell the devil you can't put this on me. I break the power of this sickness over my body. I break your power over my body! I claim the healing power of God to flow through my body to destroy this sickness in Jesus name. Glory to God for His healing Gifts.

Chapter 7
Manifestation of Healing Gifts

God's healing power is a gift from Him to us His church, (1 Corinthians 12:9) "to another the gifts of healing by the same Spirit." He makes His anointing available to remove burdens of sickness and disease and to destroy their yoke on God's people. Prophet Isaiah said "his burden shall be taken away from thy shoulder and his yoke from off thy neck, and the yoke shall be destroyed because of the anointing." In the bible, we see how Christ was going everywhere removing burdens of sicknesses and destroying yokes of diseases with His healing gift.

"How God anointed Jesus of Nazareth with the Holy Ghost and with power: who went about doing good, and healing all that were oppressed of the devil; for God was with him." (Acts 10:38)

"And Jesus went about all Galilee, teaching in their synagogues, and preaching the gospel of the kingdom, and healing all manner of sickness and all manner of disease among the people. And his fame went throughout all Syria: and they brought unto him all sick people that were taken with divers diseases and torments, and those which were possessed with devils, and those which were lunatic, and those that had the palsy; and He healed them." (Matthew 4:23-24)

Healing Gift for Leprosy

"When he was come down from the mountain, great multitudes followed him. And, behold, there came a leper and worshipped him, saying, Lord, if thou wilt, thou canst make me clean. And Jesus put forth his hand, and touched him, saying, "I will; be thou clean". And immediately his leprosy was cleansed." (Matthew 8:1-3)

When this leper came to Jesus and asked Jesus a question, if Jesus was willing to heal him, Jesus answered him yes 'I will' to heal for this is why He was anointed. He touched him and the healing power for leprosy came out of heaven to destroy leprosy in the life of this leper. Thank God for His healing gift.

Healing Gift For Fever

"And he arose out of the synagogue, and entered into Simon's house. And Simon's wife's mother was taken with a great fever; and they besought him for her. And he stood over her, and rebuked the fever; and it left her: and immediately she arose and ministered unto them." (Luke 4:38 - 39)

Jesus was anointed with the healing gift against fever and when He went to Peter's house where Peter's mother in law was sick of fever. He rebuked the fever that was oppressing her body and the fever left. The book of Matthew 8:15 says He touched her. Either way it was the healing anointing on Jesus that went to work to destroy the fever. Both Luke and Matthew say the fever left, that fever was a spirit capable of leaving. Behind every sickness and disease are spirit beings that bow to Christ's healing gift.

"And it came to pass on a certain day, as he was teaching, that there were Pharisees and doctors of the law sitting by, which were come out of every town of Galilee, and Judaea, and Jerusalem: and the power of the Lord was present to heal them." (Luke 5:17)

Healing Gift for Blind Eyes

Here, Christ was in the synagogue teaching and while teaching the healing gift on Him was present, ready to heal the sick that might make a demand of that anointing in the synagogue. A blind lady at our crusade in Alexandra, Johannesburg was brought to our crusade by her niece, she was totally blind. After ministering the word of God at the crusade. I led the people in a session of prayers according to the word preached. While we were praying the healing gift for blind eyes came into manifestation and as I heard the Holy Ghost say to me "rebuke sicknesses and diseases, rebuke blind spirit and declare blind eyes open." At an instant of that prayer, her eyes were opened and she came forward to testify with her niece who had led her to the crusade.

Healing Gift for Kidneys and Diabetes

A lady who was a member of our church branch in Olievenhoutbosch in Centurion, South Africa attended our crusade at Olievenhoutbosch listened to the message preached and when it was prayer time, as she focused on the Lord, she asked for God's healing power to help her. She said the Holy Ghost came upon her like fire and as the fire burnt inside her body she had came with a kidney failure condition, was diabetic and had high blood pressure. All of the diseases and symptoms disappeared as the healing gift of Christ fell on her.

Healing Gift for the Brain

I was ministering at Harlingen, Texas, in my friend's church when a young lady walked up to me just after I had stepped down from the pulpit to take my seat. She had seen miracles happen at that service and with her faith in the healing gift on me, approached me for prayers. She said, "I'm 16 years old and dyslexic meaning I have not been able to attend school…" and while she was talking the healing gift rose up in me and I laid my right hand on her. She fell under the power of God and within seconds saw a vision of Jesus coming to her, laid hands on her and gave her a new brain. Glory to God! Jesus put a healing gift in my right hand and I know when it's ready to undo the work of the devil. I'll always feel like there is a moving presence in my right hand. That power went straight into her brain and when she got up, she told me she saw Jesus lay His hand on her. I asked her to read what was written on the church altar and she was able to read and write the scriptures on the altar for the first time. Later she enrolled at school and has since graduated. Glory to God!

Healing Gift For Barren Wombs

Decades ago, I ministered to a lady who was barren for seven years and the healing power of God healed her womb. She brought forth twins twice as her womb was opened by the healing power of God and ended years of barrenness. Another lady who had nine miscarriages was brought to me by one of my Pastors. With compassion in my heart I ministered to her and broke the power of miscarriage and barrenness over her. She conceived afterward and gave birth to twins. If you are trusting God for children, believe God for your healing gift, claim it as yours, lay hands on your wombs, or ask your husband to regularly lay hands on your womb and command your womb to be opened, healed and fruitful by the power of God. You can also seek for an elder in the church or a minister of the gospel with the special healing gift for the womb or fruitfulness to pray for you. It could be your pastor's wife, ask them to transmit that power to your womb for healing and the blessing of babies. Don't give up if there is no immediate manifestation, keep believing and keep receiving more and more of that power through prayer. Sometimes you don't know that powers in the spirit world may be working against your fruitfulness, hence, stick to the healing gift with fervent and persistent prayer.

Healing Gift for New Ear Drum

In February 2015, I met a great Apostle of God in Lagos for prayer, he did pray for me and asked God to bless my ministry. After that meeting the healing gift for new ear drums was dropped on me. I was at a friend's church in Texas ministering when his drummer who had his eardrum removed by drug gangsters was in the service, the healing power of God overshadowed him and his hearing was restored. He came forward to testify that he could hear, before then he couldn't hear properly because he had no eardrum. The healing power of God restored it! I was in one of our churches at Mabopane, Pretoria when a lady who had five operations done to replace her eardrum that was damaged was in that meeting. I asked the congregation to put their hands on any part of their body that was sick and this lady put her hand in her ear. As we prayed, God's healing gift went right into her ear and restored the eardrum and she could hear properly after that. Praise God!

Chapter 8
Christ, the Healer

In the Old Testament, He was the healer of the Jews in the wilderness.

"…for I am the LORD that healeth thee." Exodus 15:26

"And ye shall serve the LORD your God, and he shall bless thy bread, and thy water; and I will take sickness away from the midst of thee." (Exodus 23:25)

"And the LORD will take away from thee all sickness, and will put none of the evil diseases of Egypt, which thou knowest, upon thee; but will lay them upon all them that hate thee." (Deuteronomy 7:15)

"He brought them forth also with silver and gold: and there was not one feeble person among their tribes." (Psalm 106:37)

"He sent his word, and healed them, and delivered them from their destructions." (Psalm 107:20)

"I shall not die, but live, and declare the works of the LORD." (Psalm 118:17)

"Who forgiveth all thine iniquities; who healeth all thy diseases; Who redeemeth thy life from destruction." (Psalm 103:3)

He was their guide, deliverer and healer. He led them out of Egypt and protected them in wilderness. He healed them and saved them from fiery serpents. It was Christ who followed them but they never knew. Apostle Paul writing to the church at Corinth said:

"Moreover, brethren, I would not that ye should be ignorant, how that all our fathers were under the cloud, and all passed through the sea; And were all baptized unto Moses in the cloud and in the sea; And did all eat the same spiritual meat; And did all drink the same spiritual drink: for they drank of that spiritual Rock that followed them: and that Rock was Christ." 1(Corinthians 10:1–4)

It was the healing Christ that followed them in the wilderness and in all their journey and the scripture says: There was not one feeble (weak) person among the tribes. He was their healer, He sent His word and healed them and delivered them from their destructions. He kept His covenant with Abraham and with them because their Healer, Christ was following them in the wilderness.

"My covenant will I not break, nor alter the thing that is gone out of my lips" (Psalm 89:34). CHRIST is still healing the sick in order to fulfill Prophet Isaiah's words. God spoke through prophet Isaiah:

Gifts of Healing

"Surely he hath borne our griefs, and carried our sorrows: yet we did esteem him stricken, smitten of God, and afflicted. But he was wounded for our transgressions, he was bruised for our iniquities: the chastisement of our peace was upon him; and with his stripes we are healed." (Isaiah 53:4–5)

"When the even was come, they brought unto him many that were possessed with devils: and he cast out the spirits with his word, and healed all that were sick: That it might be fulfilled which was spoken by Esaias the prophet, saying, Himself took our infirmities, and bare our sicknesses." (Matthew 8:16-17)

Christ went about healing to fulfill prophet Isaiah's prophecy.

"And Jesus went about all the cities and villages teaching in their synagogues, and preaching the gospel of the kingdom, and healing every sickness and every disease among the people." (Matthew 9:35)

"As they went out, behold, they brought to him a dumb man possessed with a devil. And when the devil was cast out, the dumb spake: and the multitudes marvelled, saying, It was never so seen in Israel." (Matthew 9:32-33)

"And great multitudes came unto him, having with them those that were lame, blind, dumb, maimed, and many others, and cast them down at Jesus' feet; and he healed them: Insomuch that the multitude wondered, when they saw the dumb to speak, the maimed to be whole, the lame to walk, and the blind to see: and they glorified the God of Israel." (Matthew 15:30-32)

"For he had healed many; insomuch that they pressed upon him for to touch him, as many as had plagues. And unclean spirits, when they saw him, fell down before him, and cried, saying, Thou art the Son of God." (Mark 3:10 – 11)

"And the whole multitude sought to touch him: for there went virtue out of him, and healed them all." (Luke 6:19)

"Now when the sun was setting, all they that had any sick with divers diseases brought them unto him; and he laid his hands on every one of them, and healed them." (Luke 4:40)

He also confirmed to them that He was CHRIST.

"The woman saith unto him, I know that Messias cometh, which is called Christ: when He is come, He will tell us all things. Jesus saith unto her, I that speak unto thee am He." (John 4:25)

PETER PREACHED CHRIST

"Therefore let all the house of Israel know assuredly, that God hath made that same Jesus, whom ye have crucified, both Lord and Christ." (Acts 2:36)

"And believers were the more added to the Lord, multitudes both of men and women. Insomuch that they brought

Gifts of Healing

forth the sick into the streets, and laid them on beds and couches, that at the least the shadow of Peter passing by might overshadow some of them. There came also a multitude out of the cities round about unto Jerusalem, bringing sick folks, and them which were vexed with unclean spirits: and they were healed every one." (Acts 5:14- 16)

"Peter said unto him, Aeneas, Jesus Christ maketh thee whole: arise, and make thy bed. And he arose immediately. And all that dwelt at Lydda and Saron saw him, and turned to the Lord." (Acts 9:34)

PHILLIP PREACHED HEALING CHRIST

Phillip who was appointed as one of the deacons to serve tables began to preach Christ.

"Therefore they that were scattered abroad went everywhere preaching the Word. Then Philip went down to the city of Samaria, and preached Christ unto them. And the people with one accord gave heed unto those things which Philip spake, hearing and seeing the miracles which he did. For unclean spirits, crying with loud voice, came out of many that were possessed with them: and many taken with palsies, and that were lame, were healed. And there was great joy in that city." (Acts 8:4–8

PAUL PREACHED HEALING CHRIST

Paul who was arrested by Christ in an encounter with Him started preaching about CHRIST.

"And there sat a certain man at Lystra, impotent in his feet, being a cripple from his mother's womb, who never had walked: The same heard Paul speak: who steadfastly beholding him, and perceiving that he had faith to be healed, Said with a loud voice, Stand upright on thy feet. And he leaped and walked." (Acts 14:8–10)

What was Paul speaking that brought faith to the lame man? It must have been about the healing Christ.

BELIEVERS MUST PREACH HEALING CHRIST

Believers were commanded to preach about the Healing Christ and to heal the sick.

"And he said unto them, Go ye into all the world, and preach the gospel to every creature." (Mark 16:15)

"Teaching them to observe all things whatsoever I have commanded you: and, lo, I am with you alway, even unto the end of the world. Amen." (Matthew 28:20)

Chapter 9
Seek God And Worship Him

If you will seek God enough He will bless you with His gifts. According to 1Corinthians 12:8, there are nine gifts of Holy Ghost and if you will seek Him enough He will cause them to manifest through you, His revelation, healing and miracle gifts. Christ has all kinds of powers which are now gifts to His body, He will decide which one to flow through you, He is such a good God. The Lord Jesus had all kinds of the power of God on Him in His earthly walk but we see in the scripture, many times where He resorted to the mountain to pray alone. Whenever He came down from the mountain, God's healing power manifested through Him as the multitudes thronged Him seeking for healing.

"And it came to pass in those days, that he went out into a mountain to pray, and continued all night in prayer to God. And when it was day, he called unto him his disciples: and of them he chose twelve, whom also he named apostles; Simon, (whom he also named Peter,) and Andrew his brother, James and John, Philip and Bartholomew, Matthew and Thomas, James the son of Alphaeus, and Simon called Zelotes, And Judas the brother of James, and Judas Iscariot, which also was the traitor. And he came down with them, and stood in the plain, and the company of his disciples, and a great multitude of people out of all Judaea and Jerusalem, and from the sea coast of Tyre and Sidon, which came to hear him, and to be healed of their diseases; And they that were vexed with unclean spirits: and they were healed. And the whole multitude sought to touch him: for there went virtue out of him, and healed them all." (Luke 6:12-19)

If you will do the same as Jesus and seek the Father regularly in prayers during the day or in the night He will reward your with His gifts.

"…and that he is a rewarder of them that diligently seek him." (Hebrews 11:6)

Seek Him today for His word, power and glory to be made manifest in you. In 2006, I had an encounter that changed my life. I had woken up early in the morning to pray and must have prayed for 5 - 6 hours in the spirit worshiping the Lord when suddenly I fell into a trance and an angel came to me and said these words to me "I'm from the Lord God Almighty, if you keep digging you will find gold". The angel then disappeared from my presence and I came back to my natural senses.

I thought of it for several days and I decided to keep digging in prayers till I increased my prayer time to 18 hours a day, just worshiping God and praying in tongues. I wanted the gold the angel told me about badly. I also got the church to join in prayer, we met daily to pray and we daily experienced the manifestation of

God's glory. Many of our people were caught in visions and they prophesied as the glory fell on them in our daily prayer meetings.

How to Seek God

"And ye shall seek me, and find me, when ye shall search for me with all your heart." (Jeremiah 29:13)

God says in His word that if you seek Him, you will find Him and He will make Himself known to you. God delights in that His people genuinely seek Him with all their hearts. The preceding verse 12 says "…and ye shall go and pray unto me, and I will hearken unto you." He is waiting to hear your call, for you to talk to Him in prayer. If you are seeking Him to heal you and give you a miracle, He will do so. Just tell Him you believe in His healing power that is able to bring you and your loved ones into good health. Show Him the chapter and verse in the bible that you believe in, your believing must be based on scriptures and not on what you think or were told. Get into the bible and search for the scriptures that reveal His healing power and pray to Him to let you experience the same in Jesus Name. If you will believe and not doubt, you will be sleeping one day only to wake up and find all your diseases have disappeared. Jesus is faithful just get into the word of God, read it to Him and tell Him that your healing is available for you under the new covenant mediated by Jesus and paid by His blood.

"Worthy is the lamb that was slain to receive power…" (Revelation 12:5)

Jesus was slain to receive power for His church and all kinds of power is available in Him. If you will seek Him and not doubt but claim the power of God over your life in the name of Jesus, it will be manifested.

"If ye abide in me, and my words abide in you, ye shall ask what ye will, and it shall be done unto you." (John 15:17)

Every believer is in Christ already and that is where you abide, but you have to work on His words to abide in you. You have to make the scriptures a part of you, cause them to be rooted in you and see them real in your spirit. Jesus said: "you shall ask what you will and it shall be done unto you" and this only takes place after His word is rooted in your spirit. Many are asking what they want from God without allowing the scriptures get into their spirit. Once the scriptures you are believing for becomes real to you, it becomes easy to believe God to perform them for you. God's will is in His Word, what He wants to do for you or has done is in His Word. Locate the scriptures and claim them as yours before asking Him to do as He has said in Jesus name.

Seek Him in Worship

Many believers go to church on Sundays to fulfill religious rite and not to worship God. Many are dry and empty of the anointing of God on their lives because they do not worship God. If you do not worship God, you will not see much of the manifestation of God's glorious power in your life. God has poured His Spirit power on the earth and in all the spirit realm. To see the power of God manifested in your life, you will have to wake up in the night while others are sleeping to worship Him or wake up early in the morning before you go to work and give Him a good worship. Tell Him you love Him, worship Him for taking your place in hell and taking away all your sicknesses and diseases, poverty, pain and rejection.

Thank Him for what He went through on the cross and appreciate Him for taking your place that you may take His place. Thank Him and worship Him for depositing His Holy Ghost in you to help you, strengthen you and bless you in your Christian walk. Sing a great song to him like David did alone in the bush while taking care of his father's sheep. Sing songs of love to Jesus. If you will do this regularly you will see your life filled with the glory of God.

Worship encounter

Years ago in the early 90's I broke the curse of lack over my life through worship. I was working as a claims manager in an insurance company with a little salary to sustain and meet my needs at that time. One Friday night, I was praying in tongues when I suddenly started worshiping God with the great song, 'blessing and hon-

or and glory and praise, and glory and praise be unto Christ the Lord". This I sang for almost five hours; in the early morning of the following day I was tired, alone in my room and I just fell on my bed to rest and take a nap. As soon as my head rested on my pillow, I fell into a trance and I saw the whole room filled with the glory of God and there was Jesus standing in a glory cloud in my room smiling and enjoying my worship. I was so scared of what I saw that my spirit left my body and it hid in the corner of the room while my body was still on the bed. I was looking at Jesus and also looking at my body on the bed, I got so scared! But He just stood in the cloud looking at me and smiling and suddenly He disappeared, and I came back to my senses. I didn't tell anyone, but kept wondering on what just happened to me. After that weekend I went to work normally not expecting any strange blessing. In the afternoon, I got a call from security downstairs in our building that someone was looking for me. When I got downstairs, an old friend I had not seen in years was waiting and told me to come to his car outside the building. He opened the boot of the car and behold the boot was filled with so many dollars I had never seen in my life.

He told me he wanted to buy properties and as an attorney I should help him buy the properties and do the documentation. I did just that for him and I was tremendously blessed financially through that transaction.

I believe Christ's visitation that weekend left me with a blessing. The curse of lack was broken! The visitation was as a result of hours of worshiping in my room alone. Worship Christ, create time to be alone with Him, to adore Him and worship Him and He will fill your life with glory.

"But the hour cometh, and now is, when the true worshipers shall worship the Father in spirit and in truth: for the Father seeketh such to worship him. God is a Spirit: and they that worship him must worship him in spirit and in truth." John 4:23 - 24

Jesus told the woman at the well that God is seeking for the true worshipers, He enjoys and longs to hear us worship Him. When you worship Him, He will cause you to experience His healing and miracle gifts.

Chapter 10
Love Walk

"A new commandment I give unto you, That ye love one another; as I have loved you, that ye also love one another. By this shall all men know that ye are my disciples, if ye have love one to another," Jesus said in John 10:34.

Do you want God's healing anointing to manifest in your life regularly? Walk in love. Refuse to walk in strife. God is love, and He left us with a commandment to love one another as He loves us. Get a revelation of the love of Jesus for you and apply the same love to your fellow human beings whether they are Christian or not.

"For God so loved the world, that he gave his only begotten Son..." (John 3:16)

God loves the people He has created and wants them to love one another but Satan brought hatred, selfishness, division, racism, wickedness, strife etc. into people's lives so that they can walk contrary to God's commandment. Jesus has commanded us to love people as He loves us. He loves us and showed it by His death on the cross. He took our sin, pain, sickness and poverty on Himself so that we may live life free of sin, pain, sickness and poverty. He went to hell and suffered the anguish and pain of hell for 72 hours so that we might end our lives in heaven, if we accept Him as Christ the Savior. Whatever He went through on earth is for our benefit, that is not selflessness, but love. He wants you to be selfless and kind to people, to forgive the people who offend you and He wants you to do good things for people. He wants you to consider other people first in all your dealings with them.

"Owe no man anything, but to love one another: for he that loveth another hath fulfilled the law." (Romans 13:8)

"Love worketh no ill to his neighbor: therefore love is the fulfilling of the law." (Romans 13:10)

What you owe your brothers and your sisters is to love them even though they may have hurt you or you don't like their faces or character. You are told to love them and that you do nothing to hurt them but be a blessing to them. Christ demands His church to walk in love, be a blessing to people. Be kind, be good, be selfless and put others first. Bear their pain, bear their weaknesses and if you do this you are a candidate for the manifestation of God's power.

Years ago I prayed for a boy who had kidney failure and I did not get results. I had prayed for others with a similar kidney problem and they were healed. So I advised them to go for the kidney transplant as scheduled. I asked God why I couldn't get results for this boy with my prayer. Later I found out that the mother and father were always in strife, which somehow had affected the boy causing the healing power not to manifest. Keep your house full of love if you want your family free from diseases and sicknesses. Don't allow strife at all! It's a major cause in families for high blood pressure, cancer, poverty etc. The bible says where there is strife their is every evil work, (James 3:16).

"But I say unto you, Love your enemies, bless them that curse you, do good to them that hate you, and pray for them which despitefully use you, and persecute you; That ye may be the children of your Father which is in heaven: for He maketh his sun to rise on the evil and on the good, and sendeth rain on the just and on the unjust." (Matthew 5:44–45)

Here, from the above scripture, we are commanded to bless those who curse us, do good to those who curse us and not to curse those who curse us, not to hate those who hate us but to repay the evil done to you with good. A dear friend of mine hurt me deeply in my time of need in the early days of my ministry. I was in pain of that hurt when the Lord told me, "Don't let that hurt take hold of you. It will hinder you, your prayers, finances and ministry. Now send money to him monthly to break the hold of that hurt on you". I did what I was told, I sent money to him every month for years. Years passed by and suddenly God used the same friend to be a connection to a mighty break though for me in ministry and up to today I am still benefiting from that break though. Glory to God! It pays to obey God; it has sweet rewards and

His mighty power will lift you up out of any mess if you will walk in love.

Apostle Paul wrote a letter to the church of God at Corinth in 1 Corinthians 13 about love. I encourage you to read and study the entire chapter.

"Love endures long and is patient and kind; love never is envious nor boils over with jealousy, is not boastful or vainglorious, does not display itself haughtily. It is not conceited (arrogant and inflated with pride); it is not rude (unmannerly) and does not act unbecomingly. Love (God's love in us) does not insist on its own rights or its own way, for it is not self-seeking; it is not touchy or fretful or resentful; it takes no account of the evil done to it [it pays no attention to a suffered wrong]. It does not rejoice at injustice and unrighteousness, but rejoices when right and truth prevail. Love bears up under anything and everything that comes, is ever ready to believe the best of every person, its hopes are fadeless under all circumstances, and it endures everything [without weakening]." 1 Corinthians 13:4-7 (AMP)

God has put His love in the heart of every believer, Romans 5:5. This love of God in us is not self-seeking, it is not touchy or resentful. Let's look at love that "it is not touchy". I know many believers today who are not experiencing the power of God as they should because they are "touchy" and "resentful". Touchy people pay attention to self and what is said or written about them but God's love in us says do not pay attention to whatever is said against you. Do not give any thought to it for it will hinder your faith and the manifestation of God's power. Touchy people are not teachable, sensitive to abusive words against them, are easily offended and difficult to correct or direct. This character traits will open the door for the enemy to get you into hurt, strife and a hardened heart. You need a soft, pliable heart that God can easily correct, direct and manifest Himself to easily. Do the Word of God, mediate on chapter 13 of first Corinthians, the Amplified version, use it to correct yourself, and get rid of the advantage Satan has had over you.

Many are sick in the body of Christ and dying, even though they have been prayed for by minsters it is difficult for them to receive their healing because of the state of their heart. Do you want constant manifestation of God's power in your life? Always walk in love, get rid of anger, strife and hurt. Do not practice racism in the church, love strangers in your country and help them, relieve the stranger, widows, orphans and watch as God blesses you tremendously.

In the scripture, Mark 7:25–29, we read the story of a Greek woman whose daughter was possessed of unclean spirits, she heard of Jesus and fell at His feet to worship Him and ask Him to help her daughter. Jesus initially refused to help this woman and called her a dog, saying that healing is children's bread and can't be given to dogs. Jesus said in verse 27 "let the children first be filled: for it is not meet to take the children's bread and cast to it unto the dogs". She replied in verse 28 "… Yes Lord yet the dogs under the table eat of the children's crumbs". Jesus replied "…for this saying go thy way; the devil is gone out of thy daughter".

God's healing and delivering power was released to heal and deliver her daughter as soon as Jesus was pleased with her faith she refused to be offended or touchy that she was called a dog. So many children of God in many churches around the world are missing out on the blessing of God by being touchy, sensitive and resentful. Some leave their churches (where God has planted them) because of offenses instead of overlooking the offence. Many are sick and dead because of offenses. Strife stops the gifts of God from manifesting. Decide to walk in love, bear the sins of others, overlook many weaknesses and stay focused on the Lord.

Samuel O. Orefuwa

OTHER BOOKS BY THE SAME AUTHOR

CONTACT INFORMATION

Word of Faith Bookshop

311 Arcadia Centre

379 Steve Biko rd

Arcadia Pretoria

0083

South Africa

Tel: 012 326 87830

Samuel O. Orefuwa

info@wof-ministries.com

www.wof-ministries.com

Gifts of Healing

Gifts of Healing

Samuel O. Orefuwa

www.ingramcontent.com/pod-product-compliance
Lightning Source LLC
Chambersburg PA
CBHW051710090426
42736CB00013B/2632